Painting French Dolls

with China Painting Techniques

by Neva Wade Garnett

Jumeau (called Lyric): Head circumference 9½in (24.2cm), lambskin wig, 16in (40.6cm) tall on ball [jointed] body.

Published By

HOBBY HOUSE P
Cumberland, Maryl

DEDICATION

With love to my mother, Clara Wade,
and to my daughter and best friend,
Dona Garnett Kizziar.

Photographs by McGill photography, Paradise, California.

All dolls shown are made by the author.
Costumes by Shirley Darmohray
unless otherwise indicated.

A special Thank You to my friends and customers who loaned their dolls for photography.

Rosemary Paciotti, Isabelle Benedetti, Rita Neary,
Shirley Darmohray, Darlynne McKillop, Dorian Fernandez,
Leora Wreede, Arleene Wimple, Vivian Fry

Neva Wade Garnett

Additional copies of this book may be purchased at $12.95
plus $1.75 postage/handling from
HOBBY HOUSE PRESS, INC.
900 Frederick Street, Cumberland, Maryland 21502

ISBN: 0-87588-245-5

Table of Contents

Introduction

As a child I was not very interested in dolls. I was far too busy swinging from the trees playing "Tarzan," or playing baseball with the neighborhood boys.

The only doll I can recall playing with was a *Betsy Wetsy*. This was a rubber baby doll created for loving and "mothering." I had named it after a boy cousin, Bobby Bruce, whom I disliked. Often, this poor doll received a sound slapping and shaking as I scolded.

A small hole in the mouth accommodated a little nursing bottle. I never used the bottle. Rather, I poked a sample of everything I had on my dinner plate into the mouth of this poor doll. Sometimes it was juice, mashed potatoes, gravy, you name it. If I ate it, "he" got a bite, too. Of course, after a time, this rubber baby began smelling terribly. My mother finally disposed of this badly decomposed doll.

It was after I had married and moved to New England that my appetite for dolls was whetted. My mother, Clara Wade, was employed at that time by Emma Clear of the Humpty-Dumpty Doll Hospital located in Redondo Beach, California. Mrs. Clear was the pioneer of American doll reproduction. Mother wrote to me about the beautiful dolls that were brought to the Clear's establishment for restoration. It was from her extensive experience as the Clear's restoration artist that her vast store-house of doll knowledge was attained.

Eventually, the Humpty-Dumpty Doll Hospital changed hands but Mother remained in the employ of the new owner, Lillian Smith, for some time. When the establishment left the area, my mother decided to go into the restoration business for herself. She had earned a marvelous reputation for her method of invisible repair. Even under a magnifyer, her restorations could not be detected. She restored many rare and beautiful dolls for museums.

It was satisfied collectors who loaned their valuable dolls for mold making, sometimes in exchange for the restoration fee. This is how many of her original molds were obtained at a time before the commercial doll molds were available. Many of the lovely "Clear" heads were given to my mother by "Mama Clear," as she was called by her friends. At a later date, these, too, were utilized for mold making to reproduce the enchanting "Clear" type dolls.

My father's health was failing. The heavy sea air did not agree with his condition. A high, dry climate was suggested by his doctor. They had friends living here in Paradise, California, and, after a visit, they decided it was, indeed, "Paradise." Beautiful lakes and streams abound. Both being avid fishermen, they decided Paradise was the location for them! I suspect Paradise's high, dry climate (that the doctor ordered) was simply a bonus.

After settling in, they got down to the business of the restorations that had started piling up. Restoring dolls is difficult, grueling work. Mother had about had her fill of it after so many years. Meanwhile, the mold making process of dolls began. Eventually, Mother gave up her restorations and went into doll production.

I had no inkling that Mother had attained so much prestige in the "doll world." I was impressed and fascinated. Art had always been my passion since I was old enough to hold a pencil, and I had dabbled in many medias. I particularly enjoyed doing pastel portraits of children. I loved the softly curved cheek, the expressive lips and, sometimes, mischevious eyes. It was a real challenge to attempt to capture the "personality" of each child, along with a good likeness. It was very gratifying, and my experience in this area has served me well in my doll making career.

When I observe children, I am apt to compare them to certain dolls I make. When I first reproduced the pensive A. Marque doll, I never thought I would ever see a child with such unusual features and expression. Indeed, I did! As a friend, another doll artist, and I were sitting in a cafeteria, there, before our very eyes, at another table, was the A. Marque doll ALIVE and eating his custard with zest.

Illustration 1. *Thank You for My Present: Jumeau (called Lyric): Head circumference 9½in (24.2cm), lambskin wig, 16in (40.6cm) tall on ball-jointed body. Costume — Dona Kizziar.*

We could not take our eyes off him. He was so beautiful he could have as easily been a fragile little girl. I am sure other doll artists have experienced the same surprised delight in spotting real, live dolls.

Our decision to move to California came at a time when my husband was considering leaving his profession in golf. It seemed an opportune time to make a change and the move to Paradise would enable me to be near, and learn the art of doll making from one of the best, my mother, Clara Wade. For any success I may have experienced in doll artistry, I must thank my mother. It was her encouragement, patience and devotion to her art that enabled me to learn this very exacting and exhausting business of doll reproduction. She is a perfectionist and would accept only the best from me. She taught me to accept only my best.

Clara's Doll Hospital was not exactly modern. Indeed, in winter, like Mama Clear's shop of the past, a potbellied wood stove warmed us. Since I was seated away from it, my feet would get so cold that I would sit with them in a cardboard box for warmth. At one time, several other ladies were employed at "Clara's." It was a friendly place to work and we really were like a family.

Although there is no need to be, my parents are of a frugal nature, having weathered the great depression of the 1920s. In winter, when the kiln would be "cooking" dolls, a savory stew could be simmering on the closed lid of the kiln. Coming to work early in the morning, the girls would sniff the air and ask, "What's cookin' on the kiln today?" When I decided it was time to go into business for myself, I knew I would miss the warm, homey atmosphere of Clara's Doll Hospital.

I felt unsure for some time and would ask Mother to critique my dolls. Eventually, as my business expanded, my confidence grew. I learned to rely on my own instincts and to employ the teachings of my mother.

Sometimes, now, a customer from the East Coast, visiting here in the West, will call and ask if they may tour my "factory." I laughingly advise them that my "factory" consists of one 8ft (2.4m) by 10ft (3m) workroom, a garage, a bureau drawer and a shoe box. This is true and a perfect example of "making do." Of course, when I first started, I never dreamed that 20 years would pass so quickly. I always intended to expand my working area but I got so used to working in a closet, so to speak, that to change it seemed a waste of time and money. Contrary to belief, one does not require a large building to produce an impressive number of dolls. Of course, it would be nice, but not necessary, in my opinion.

I suspect much of the doll work produced today is done on the kitchen table.

There are times when, if I were to be perfectly candid, I would admit I feel burned out. The stress that can accompany this type of work can be hard to live with after 20 years. Yet, for most of the time, I approach each day with enthusiasm. Every new doll I reproduce results in a love affair with that single doll until another, even more beautiful doll, is available. Today, such wonderful doll molds and supplies are at the fingertips of all doll artists. How different from when my mother started.

Doll collectors are a special breed. I cannot begin to count the wonderful friendships that have sprung from my doll business. I have found that honesty in all cases is the best and only policy. If I am going to be late with delivery, I admit it and reveal the reason why. Some doll makers feel it is demeaning to disclose that they are having problems. I disagree. It is when you are evasive, that doll customers will press you because they cannot be sure you are to be trusted.

The following pages of this book are devoted to assisting the aspiring doll artist in the area of most difficulty, painting. The secret to my success with line work is simply the way I grip my brushes, control and knowing how the doll is supposed to look.

Illustration 2. *Bru Jne 8: Head circumference 9½in (24.2cm), lambskin wig, 17in (43.2cm) tall on ball-jointed body.*

Illustration 3. *I've Got a Secret:* **Left:** *Cody Jumeau (unmarked): Head circumference 14in (35.6cm), synthetic hair wig, 26in (66cm) tall on ball-jointed body.* **Right:** *Cody Jumeau (unmarked): Head circumference 14in (35.6cm), human hair wig, 26in (66cm) tall on ball-jointed body.*

Illustration 4. Sisters: **Left:** *Bru Jne 10 Oriental/ head circumference 12in (30.5cm), human hair wig, 24in (61cm) tall on kid body with bisque limbs.* **Right:** *Bru Jne 10 Oriental/ with molded teeth, head circumference 12in (30.5cm), human hair wig, 22in (55.9cm) tall on ball-jointed body.*

Illustration 5. Oriental Bru Jne 10: Head circumference 12in (30.5cm), human hair wig, 24in (61cm) tall on kid body with bisque limbs.

Illustration 6. *Oriental Bru Jne 10, with molded teeth: Head circumference 12in (30.5cm), human hair wig, 22in (55.9cm) tall on ball-jointed body.*

Illustration 7. *Madame Butterfly: Steiner FA 15/ head circumference 11in (27.9cm), human hair wig, 22in (55.9cm) tall on ball-jointed body. Costume — Vivian Fry.*

Illustration 8. *Bru Jne 10: Head circumference 12in (30.5cm), human hair wig, 24in (61cm) tall on kid body with bisque shoulder plate and lower bisque arms.*

Illustration 9. *Suki: SFBJ French (character) Pouty 252/ head circumference 9½in (24.2cm), human hair wig, 15in (38.1cm) tall on ball-jointed body. Costume — made in Alaska. Arctic fox, seal skin and rabbit fur.*

14

Illustration 10. *SFBJ French (character) Pouty 252: Head circumference 9½in (24.2cm), human hair wig, 15in (38.1cm) tall on ball-jointed body.*

Illustration 11. *I Love Little Bunnie: A 14T/ head circumference 13in (33cm), synthetic wig, 24in (61cm) tall on ball-jointed body.*

Foreword —

Ten Steps to Success

1. Carefully read the "How To" section.
2. Examine the black and white "study" photographs and eyelash and brow sketches.
3. Study (a) slant, (b) swing, (c) spacing, (d) length.
4. With medium felt tip, black pen on white paper, draw a crescent shape. Holding your pen in your usual manner for writing; familiarize yourself with a, b, c, d, by stroking upper and lower lashes onto your crescent shape. Utilize this shape as though it were the upper and/or lower curve of a cut out eye socket. For the upper lashes, turn the paper upside down — as you will the doll head. Always stroke lashes toward you! NEVER away from you. At this point, thin strokes are not important. It is a, b, c and d that you are striving for.
5. Take your "eye" brush No. 000. Be sure you are gripping the brush as described in the "How To" text. Study the photographic illustration of the hand and brush until you can duplicate the grip exactly. It will feel awkward at first, but in time you will be very comfortable with it and you will experience wonderful control.
6. When you feel comfortable holding your brush, proceed again to your white paper. Using the black paint you have previously mixed, stroke onto the paper at random just to familiarize yourself with the action of the brush and paint.

    Now, try for thin, slanted strokes, using the paint and media in the manner described in the text. Do not worry; it takes practice. Relax!
7. Again, draw the crescent shape and with your brush and paint; stroke lashes onto it just as though it were an eye socket. Turn your paper to accommodate your brush and fingers to maintain a smooth stroke, and your strokes will slant and swing more effortlessly. When you paint the head, you will find it easier to achieve good results if you remember to rotate the head. You will soon get the feel of when it is necessary to rotate the head, as your fingers will be restricted if you do not!
8. Repeat this routine for the brows. Experiment by pulling some strokes toward you and stroking others away from you, (unlike lashes which are stroked only toward you). You can tell which direction to stroke, by "doing." Also, some strokes will be made holding the head upside down. I use a combination of all for brows — stroking toward — and away — holding the head upside down and right side up!
9. Study the lip photographs and sketches. On your paper, and freehand, try sketching different lip shapes. Watch for (a) placement, (b) shape, (c) size. Remember to review the text concerning spaces and comparisons.
10. When you have completed these practice exercises, paint your doll, referring from time to time to the photographs, sketches and text. Remember, do not be discouraged. It will work for you if you persevere. When you feel frustrated, get up, gaze out a window, walk around, stretch, and you will feel more relaxed.

    You will see improvement, perhaps slow at first, but it will come! My students tell me the rewards far outnumber the frustrations and they are correct!

An afterthought:

This is so important and I almost forgot to mention it! The fingernail of your fourth finger must be trimmed very short to enable you to "anchor" it, and hold the brush in a more or less vertical position. (See hand/brush photograph.) A long nail will prevent the correct positioning of your brush.

Painting the French Doll

So — you would like to make a doll — Good! Since commercial molds are now available, anyone who has a longing to make their very own doll can. However, there are two important requirements. I call them the big P's, PAINTING and PERSEVERANCE!

It is true, that casting and dumping the mold, cleaning greenware and cutting the eye sockets are important. These processes require some practice, but it is not there that the beginner (as well as advanced) doll maker seems to experience the most difficulty.

My theory is, to be successful and authentically paint a doll, you must first learn to recognize the special effect the original maker attained by stroking and blending the paints in a certain way or style. Although the style of one antique doll maker's painting may mimic that of another to a degree, there is a "special look" that separates one style of painting from another. Sometimes the shape of the brow, lips or lashes will help to identify an unmarked doll.

Since no two dolls (even from the same mold) will ever be painted exactly alike, we are allotted a degree of freedom. Even the antiques of the same model vary in expression and style, somewhat. No one person seems to have painted the head in its entirety, since these dolls were processed in a production line. Because you will be painting the complete head, you must recognize not just the style, but the process by which these effects were attained.

In my painting seminars, I use a simplified method of determining this. I analyze the style of painting by breaking it down to the simplest forms, or designs. I feel that before you can paint features successfully, you must be able, first, to draw them. Many artists feel they paint better than they draw and, therefore, do not attach much importance to the structure of a feature. However, the correct shape and size is of utmost importance in attaining the desired effect.

The sketches contained in this manual should help you to determine how a certain shape can be identified by reducing it down to a primary form and continuing from there. These sketches are not intended to be classified as artistic works or finished drawings. Rather, they are a means to an end, being basic and freehand — in some cases oversimplified to make a point clear. Study them carefully. Place transparent paper over them and trace over them to get the feel, if necessary. Do not be discouraged if your results are not perfect at first. Practice and a real desire are your keys to success.

Using my method, you will soon realize full control over your brush. That is important. Then, as your confidence grows, so will your ability. Most important, enjoy it. Though it is a labor, it should be a labor of love!

Good luck!

Flesh tones

Using a rather wide brush, I paint a wash, consisting of paint and media (oil) over the entire head. It is not important to be very fussy here, as it will be almost completely wiped off later. Be sure you have enough pigment if you want a high, rosy complexion. For a very pale doll, use less pigment and more media.

I usually paint four to six heads (medium size) at one time. By the time the last head is painted, the first should be ready to wipe, but do not rush it. You must allow time for the color to "soak in."

Using clean, lint-free, china silk, I wipe off all the wash, being careful to wipe out ears, nostrils and any creases. Be careful; the paint will puddle in these areas. Do not wipe the head bone-dry, but just so it has a slightly "tacky" feel. It will shine softly, not oily, but just a soft patina. This is when the cheek paint should be applied. *Note:* Some people prefer to fire the head before applying the cheek paint. That is acceptable and safer, but will involve an extra firing. Really, with a bit of practice, you can blend the cheek paint right into the flesh coat. The result will be a smooth, blended cheek with no ugly streaks, light spots or harsh edges. It does take practice, so do not be discouraged.

Cheeks

With a ball of lamb's wool about the size of a walnut wrapped in china silk, I pounce into the concentrated flesh color. Blot the pouncer by pressing it lightly a few times on a clean, white plate or platter. Now, apply a patch of paint with the pouncer onto the center of the cheek. Immediately, start padding outward and upward, trying to keep your pouncing pressure even. The more pressure exerted, the more paint the pouncer will lift off so, at first, I pounce rather gently and evenly outward and upward from the center. When the cheek is well covered and I have the tint I desire, I use a larger, clean pouncer to softly pounce all over the head. After I have evenly pounced the forehead, chin and so forth, I will, again, gently pounce the whole cheek area with this "seasoned" pouncer. The first pouncer will be laden with paint. This second pouncer will be only slightly soiled with just a little paint and oil picked up from the rest of the head.

After firing, if I am unhappy with the color or blend, it is possible to go over it before the next firing, using the same process.

Lashes

Lashes should be artfully rendered. It is not imperative that they be terribly thin. More important is the slant and spacing of the strokes. Try to space them as evenly as possible by applying a tiny dot on the eye socket where you feel each lash should be placed to correspond with the lash before it. Avoid stiff, too straight strokes. Keep your paint black and "inky." I tell my students, "Think Ink." Too much media will either bleed or create a washy, pale gray lash. Most French dolls' eyelashes were painted similarly, so the basic, planted stroke is acceptable for most. The exception may be certain Jumeaus. Their eyelashes, sometimes, are longer and, in some cases, have a more pronounced "swing." Baby dolls' lashes differ too, being shorter and straighter but, for the most part, the French doll artists used a pretty general technique.

Brows

Study and compare spaces and shapes. Measure distances from one point to another. That is the secret of successfully finding the proper placement and shape of the brow.

The brows of old dolls appear to be structured from a simple one-stroke arch or crescent design. After blending the paint in a pleasing manner, fine brush strokes are utilized to produce a finished, artistic look. Proper placement of the arch and the finishing brush strokes will help determine the style and expression of the completed doll.

Too heavy an application of pigment, as well as a timid approach, can spoil the appearance of an otherwise fine doll.

Hint

Always shade upward into the feathered strokes, not too high, or you will lose those thin, lovely strokes. Never paint a solid mass across the arch, then hope you can pull the fine strokes from it. This can result in a harsh, amateurish looking brow. Fire the brows twice, trying to accomplish most of the shape and feathering the first firing, but do not go "over board" as you can touch up and refine the fired existing brows before the final firing.

Lips

Most lips are a modified heart shape. To determine the shape of the lips, I "look for the heart." Then, I decide where the heart shape has been changed to represent the final shape of the lip.

Observe the relationship of the space from

the mouth to the nose — the length, depth and modeling. Also, watch the placement of the lips, being positive they are placed exactly under the center of the nose. It is so easy to misplace the lips in our zest to get everything else going. Some lips were not painted to follow the modeled mouth contour so do not slavishly paint the complete modeled area unless the antique was done in that manner. Many replicas look as though they have a "fat lip" because the mouth is too fully painted. The lower lip, in particular, is a target for this common error in judgment.

There are always exceptions, but the finer French dolls have rather pale, soft looking lips, with the deeper color being reserved for the lovely, expressive accent lines placed on the top and bottom edges of the lips. Decide the shape these accent lines should be. They were not always painted the same and the placement may be different, one doll from another. The center (or dividing) line also is darker to enhance the lovely modeling of the lips. Usually, you will find a subtle shading of deeper color on the upper section of the lower lip, just under the dividing line. This shading should be well blended and not harsh.

Before the final firing, you may wish to "gussy-up" your first painting. It has been fired and it is safe to go over it and refine the areas, where needed. Remember, at this point you can add paint, but once it has been fired you cannot remove (safely) the fired pigment. Rather than over paint the first time around, I suggest you paint with some caution knowing you can later touch up your fired work.

Before your final firing, you will examine your work carefully for flaws. Does the brow color need to be deepened at the base? Is more feathering needed for reshaping? Now is the time to add those lip accent lines and any shading needed on the mouth.

Pad on a soft lavender color (pale, of course) under the brows. Blend it smoothly and subtly. It should be kept natural looking. Many of the lovely, high-priced French antiques had this shading. It does add to the charm of the doll and brings the eyes to life!

Now, carefully paint a thin black line around the inside edge of the eye socket. Do not use your paint too fluid here, or it will bleed onto your lashes in a most unattractive way. This line serves to frame the lovely glass eyes that you will set in later.

Look over the head carefully for smudges of unwanted paint, or anything you may have overlooked.

Remember

All my china colors are diluted by dipping the tip of my brush into lacquer thinner, then into the oil. Now stroke through your paint while rolling your brush. Blot excess moisture on a white paper, then paint.

Caution

Lacquer thinner is toxic and flammable. It should never be inhaled or ingested. Keep a small bottle or jar with a tight lid, to be closed, except when dipping into it. It evaporates rapidly so you must work at a steady pace, reloading your brush often.

Practice this method. You will find your line work, especially, will flow off your brush more readily without the discouraging "dragging" that you may experience using oil (media) only. This method was revealed to my mother, Clara Wade, when she was employed by Emma Clear of Humpty-Dumpty Hospital.

It works!!

You are probably aware that china paints also are toxic. Keep your hands clean and wash off any that accumulate on your fingers. Do not "point" your brush with your lips. Rather, wet your fingers with saliva and point with your fingers.

A tip

To remove a small amount of unfired

paint, saliva works great. Wet a clean Q-tip with it and clean off the area. A toothpick can also be used to correct <u>small</u> mistakes, such as, a single lash or eyebrow stroke. To erase a complete brow, lips and so forth, dip a Q-tip into the lacquer thinner, blot off the excess and wipe the paint off. Follow with a clean Q-tip wet with saliva. If you must eliminate a <u>large</u> painted area, I recommend scrubbing the whole face thoroughly with hot water, detergent and a stiff brush. <u>Be sure</u> to rinse thoroughly inside the head and out several times to eliminate <u>any</u> soap residue. Pat dry with a lint-free cloth. Then you can start over.

Are your ready? "FIRE!!"

Brush Technique

The reason I am comfortable with my brush is because I exert complete control over it. The way I grip the brush is even more important than the size or type of brush I use. Strictly a finger movement is used for my lash and brow strokes. I do not allow my brush or hand to "float." I practically glue the fourth and fifth fingers together while resting the brush across the thumb and first finger. The third finger grips the brush down very low, almost at the bristles. The fourth and fifth (little) finger are resting against each other, even though the fourth finger is usually my pivot (or anchor) finger. This finger stabilizes my hand, gives me leverage, but allows my fingers free movement while yet restricting my wrist. It is most important to remember that <u>your fingers</u> do the work. I do not utilize a loose flowing stroke. Rather, my brush strokes are tightly controlled, while at the same time experiencing enough freedom to "swing" or curve them in an artistic manner.

It is important with this type of brush technique to learn to hold and rotate the head in such a way that you are not constantly lifting and changing the position of your hand or fingers. Rather, allow the head as you move it, to accommodate your hand and brush. <u>Of course</u>, you <u>will</u> move the position of your hand from time to time, but turning the head will eliminate a lot of hand positioning.

Some of the features are painted upside down, especially the upper lashes and some of the brow strokes. Holding the head upside down is an excellent way to judge your work. A lopsided mouth or uneven brows will really show up. Also, observe your work in a mirror. This gives you an objective picture of your overall work. As one's eyes tire and patience is frayed, it is easy to overlook an otherwise obvious mistake.

The brushes I use are not especially fine. It is the <u>point</u> of the brush that enables one to paint a thin line. A brush with only a few hairs does not lend itself well to my style of painting. Indeed, my students are surprised when I demonstrate the fine stroking that can be coaxed from a short, stubby brush with a good point.

The care of your favorite brushes is important. I treat my "pets" like an old friend whom I may always count on. Always clean your brushes well and do not leave any paint on them to dry and spoil a good point. If the hairs "splay out," I simply clean the brush in lacquer thinner dip the tip in media, point it, then lay it aside to rest.

Kiln Firings

I was not going to mention kiln firings because all kilns are accompanied by an instruction manual. Types of firings and schedules will vary with the size and style of kiln and the load you are firing. However, upon second thought, I am sure many bad china paint colors are the direct result of an under- or over-fired kiln. By over firing, I am referring to a single firing episode that has fired too long a period of time. Under firing, of course, is the opposite.

Browns will sometimes fade and turn muddy with over firing. Reds may have a bluish undertone, especially those with gold base. Underfiring creates a brickish color.

To achieve the best results from your paints and firings, be careful not to apply the paint too heavily. A watercolor wash is the way I sometimes describe the body of the paint as I apply it. If a deeper color is needed, it is usually wise to fire between coats, adding more color each time. However, some paints do not stand up to repeated firings, so caution here must be exercised. My total china paint firings, per head, usually number three. The first is the flesh coat and cheeks. The second is the lashes, brows, lips, eye dots and nostrils. The third is what I call my touch-up firing. At this point, I will deepen the coloring, add shading to the lips, plus accent lines and any other areas that need attention before this, my final firing. The lavender shading under the brow and the black eye rim is done at this time, also.

It is imperative, especially with an over-glaze (china paint) firing, to use two cones. I use a Junior (small) cone in the automatic shut off (called a kiln sitter). This is strictly a back-up cone in case you forget and leave your kiln unattended. The Senior (large) cone is a visual cone placed near a peek hole where you may observe it. Shutting off the kiln when the Senior (large) cone has matured is important to avoid over firing or under firing. When the cone bends to a perfect arch, the desired temperature within the kiln should have been reached, so watch that Senior cone. It bends very quickly toward the end of the firing time. The Junior (small) cone is not always dependable, even when carefully set.

The paints I recommend are fired to 018 degrees Fahrenheit. For heavier gold base colors, a higher fire may be desired. Usually, the china paint manufacturer will indicate the Fahrenheit temperature required to mature their paints.

Though firing schedules vary, I will disclose the schedule I find suitable for my kiln and paints: Start on Medium with lid propped open. Fire for one hour; turn to high and shut the lid. Proceed to fire until the Senior cone indicates it has matured. Total firing time, approximately two hours.

This very simple schedule works well for me. Your kiln may recommend a different schedule. Read your manual carefully. It is time well spent.

About Color

Pre-mixed paints can be purchased in small pots. I prefer to mix my own dry pigment for several reasons: You are limited to just a few colors. You are at the mercy of the consistency of the pre-mix, which is usually much too oily. Often, it contains minute granules that refuse to dissolve or blend out.

If you must use pre-mixed paints, I will recommend colors that I have used and found to be acceptable. I do not mention brands, as these will vary state to state.

Pre-mixed Gloss Colors:

Cheek and **Flesh** — Pompadour Red or Light Pompadour Red.

Lips — The same Pompadour Red color, but diluted to a pale color.

Lashes — Outlining Black.

Brows — Red-Brown and Hair Brown. Use caution. Do not apply too strong. The results can be harsh and garish. Use these browns separately, or mixed together to obtain satisfactory brow color.

Dry pigment Gloss that I use:

Address: Willoughby's China Paint Company
Shingle Springs, California 95682

Cheek and **Flesh** No. 327 — Dull Red — A deep rosy red with no orange or brown undertone. Dependable!

Lips — The same Dull Red, but diluted to a soft, pale pink.

Expression Lines — Dull Red used quite deep for accent.

Eye Shadow — Small amount of Dull Red mixed with Baby Blue for a soft, grayish lavender color.

Lashes — Outlining Black, a rich pure black that lends itself to fine line work.

Brows — No. 321 Dark Brown, a cold dark brown with no warm undertones. For blondes it can be diluted and used as is, or mixed with Yellow Brown for warmth. For brunettes, use full strength, diluting only enough so it will flow.

No. 27 Yellow Brown, a rich gold-blonde. Dilute it for a pale gold-blonde. Full strength, it fires to a bright gold-blonde. These colors mature at 018 (Fahrenheit) cone.

Note: To dilute the colors, dip brush into pen oil and thinner. Combine with the paint and mix until the color has thinned out to the desired tint. Dilute just a small amount at a time as you use it.

Media No. 2 — For diluting concentrated pigment such as the flesh wash.

Pen Oil — For fine line work and feature painting.

Pouncing Lamb's Wool can be purchased at the drug store. China silk squares are available from most china paint supplies or may be bought by the yard at a silk outlet store.

Lacquer-Thinner may be found at most paint or hardware stores. Use only pure thinner, never acrylic thinner.

Brushes Grumbacher

No. 7701 — size 1/2in (1.3cm) (flat) for applying the flesh wash.

No. 7703 — size 000 for line work, fine strokes.

No. 7704 — size 4 for lips and brow shading.

These three brushes enable me to paint any size head. Of course, you may wish to purchase other sizes, but I find these suitable for my style of painting. They are of good quality and dependable.

Let's Elaborate

Brows

Remember, before you attempt to paint features, first analyze the shapes by breaking them down to their simplest forms. Then compare spaces. This is so important in observing the relationship of one shape to another and determining correct placement. One measurement I am very careful of is the distance from the upper eyelid to the under section of the brow. Careful study of the shape of this space will help determine if one eyebrow compares favorably to the other. Keep in mind, most of us are not ambidexterous so one brow will be easier to place correctly and to stroke artistically. I start with the "easy" brow. By comparing first the space between the upper eyelid to the under side of the brow, I determine if the second brow is comparing favorably. Because we are not duplicating machines, the two brows are seldom perfectly matched, (notice the antiques) but they should at least look as though they belong on the same face. Another helpful comparison is to draw an imaginary line straight across one brow through the other brow to determine if they line up. Do this on the upper and lower sections of the brow, also, the inside and outside corners.

Lashes

You will discover with practice the lashes will get easier. You may find that getting the same slant or swing on both the left and right eyes can be a problem. Do not be overly concerned. The eyes of beautiful antique French dolls are seldom painted identically and I assume "they" had the same problem. The first lash on the inside corner can be a helpful guide for correct slant. If this first lash is not well placed, the rest of the lashes that follow may look stiff and out of line. This first slanted lash will enable you to more easily get the correct stroke going without a lot of correcting.

Mouth

I approach the painting of the mouth by studying the distance from the bottom of the nose to the lip. Then I determine the overall shape by imagining a heart shape, and how the top lip is formed as compared to the heart. I study the dip in the center of the top lip, too. Is it close to the center dividing line of the mouth, or is it on the high side? Do the corners of the lips turn up, or are they squared off? This can be determined in part by first placing the center dividing line through the lips. This line actually decides the up or down turn of the corners of the lips. Notice, also, if there is a single center line, indicating a closed mouth, or if there are two lines, as in lips slightly parted, or open. Be sure to check the fullness of the lower lip and the shape, the depth and width especially. Check the accent lines for correct placement. These little expression lines can make a difference in the overall shape of the finished lips.

Remember — Take time to analyze the features of the doll or photographs which you will use as a model to paint from.

On the following pages you will find close-up photographs of eyes, brows and lips of popular French dolls. Because some of the dolls were quite small, the photographs have been enlarged many times for good detail. Please keep in mind that minute particles of wax in eye corners and minor flaws not visible to the naked eye have been magnified.

You will also find study sketches which I have done to illustrate some of the points I wish to impress upon you.

Practice makes perfect so do not worry if you are not successful at first. As in all worthwhile things, the results will be well worth the effort.

If you will diligently follow my suggestions and learn to observe, either by careful examination of the antique doll, or a very good, clear photograph, you will soon be able to discern the various "steps" that will lead you to the beautiful and authentic finish.

This simplified method of approaching the feature painting was explained and demonstrated to me by my mother, Clara Wade. It is my desire to pass it on to you — my friends.

Neva's Recipe For Grinding Dry, Overglaze Pigment By The Vial

*P*lace small amounts of dry pigment on a grinding plaque (approximately one teaspoonful). With a pallet knife, grind firmly into the glass plaque using the <u>rough</u> side of the plaque. Scrape aside. Repeat the process until all the pigment is thoroughly ground. For gold base colors, (many reds and roses) one hour per vial of grinding is considered usual.

Scrape together into a pile in the center of the plaque. Add by the drop, <u>French Fat Oil</u> and, as you do, chop down through the pigment and mash and scrape, adding fat oil until enough has been added to <u>moisten</u> (not wet) it. It should be a <u>crumbly</u> consistency such as dry pie crust dough, with a slight moisture showing through. Add <u>mixing</u> or <u>painting</u> media (not pen oil, cobaiba, lavender oil, and so forth) a little at a time, mashing and scraping up until it appears the consistency of <u>mashed potatoes</u> or heavy butter. It should hold a shape when scraped into a pile such as a <u>soft</u> mound.

Too much media will result in a runny consistency. If this occurs, you must grind and add more <u>dry</u> pigment; or, let it "sit" until some of the oil evaporates. (This sometimes takes weeks.) Hint: during the last grinding process (using the media) if it appears not to want to "break down," add a few drops of <u>lacquer thinner</u>. This final grinding of pigment and oils should be done for at least one-half hour, especially if the pigment is gold based (reds).

Note: Some brands of paint do not require as much grinding but better safe, than sorry!

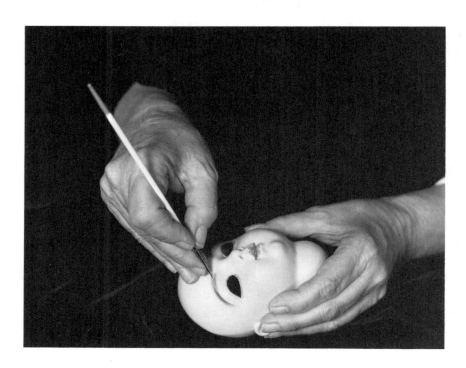

Illustration 1. Gripping the brush.

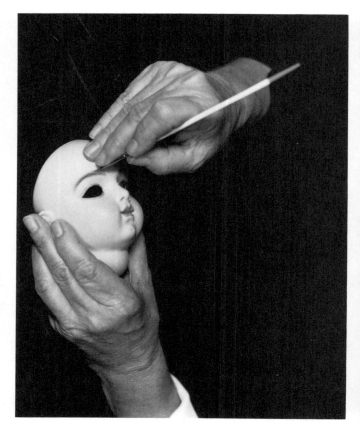

Illustration 2. Adding strokes to shape brow.

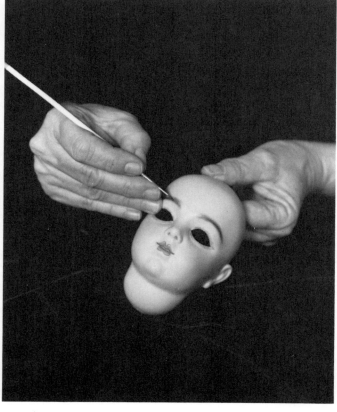

Illustration 3. Touch-up painting — adding shadow.

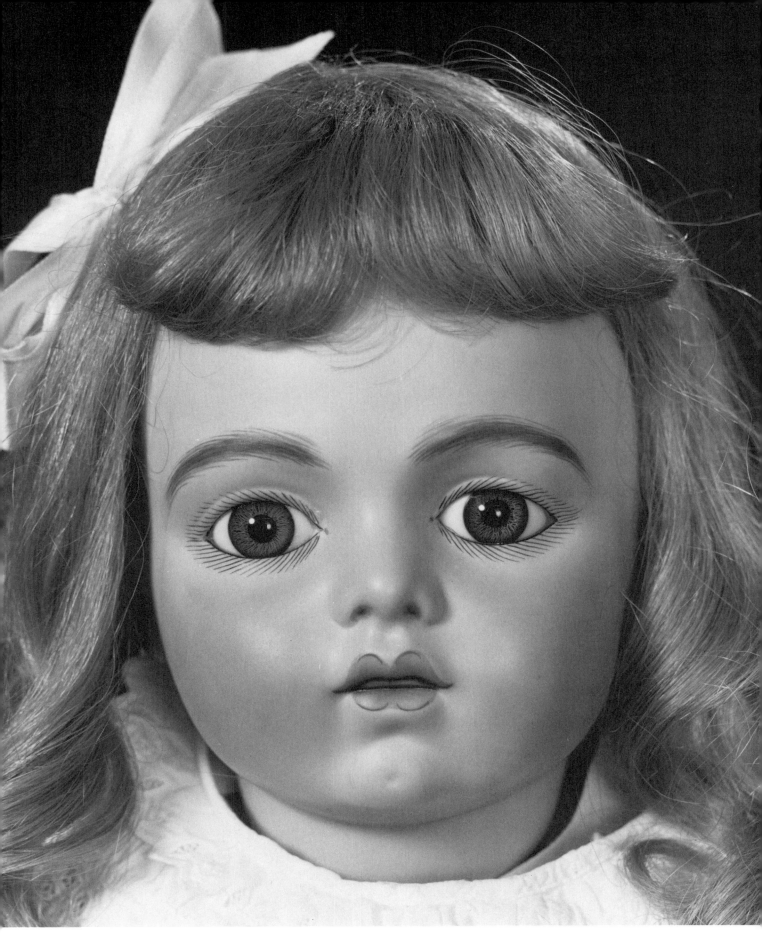

Illustration 4. Bru Jne 13.

Illustration 5. Steiner F A 15.

Illustration 6. Tête Jumeau.

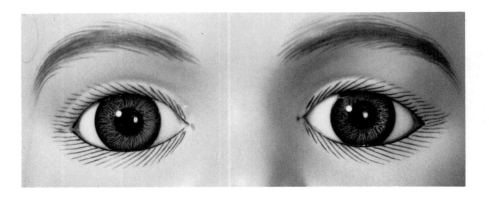 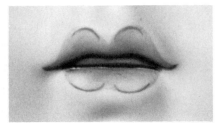

Illustration 7. Bru Jne 13/ eyes, lips.

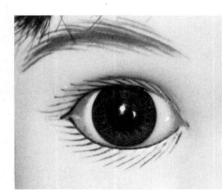 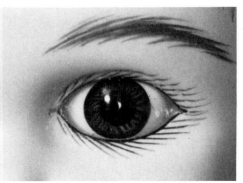 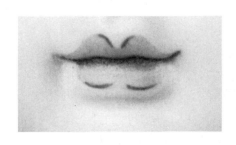

Illustration 8. Steiner F A 15/ eyes, lips.

  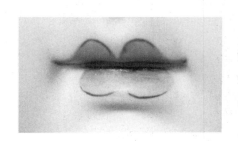

Illustration 9. Tête Jumeau/ eyes, lips.

Illustration 10. *F. G. in scroll.*

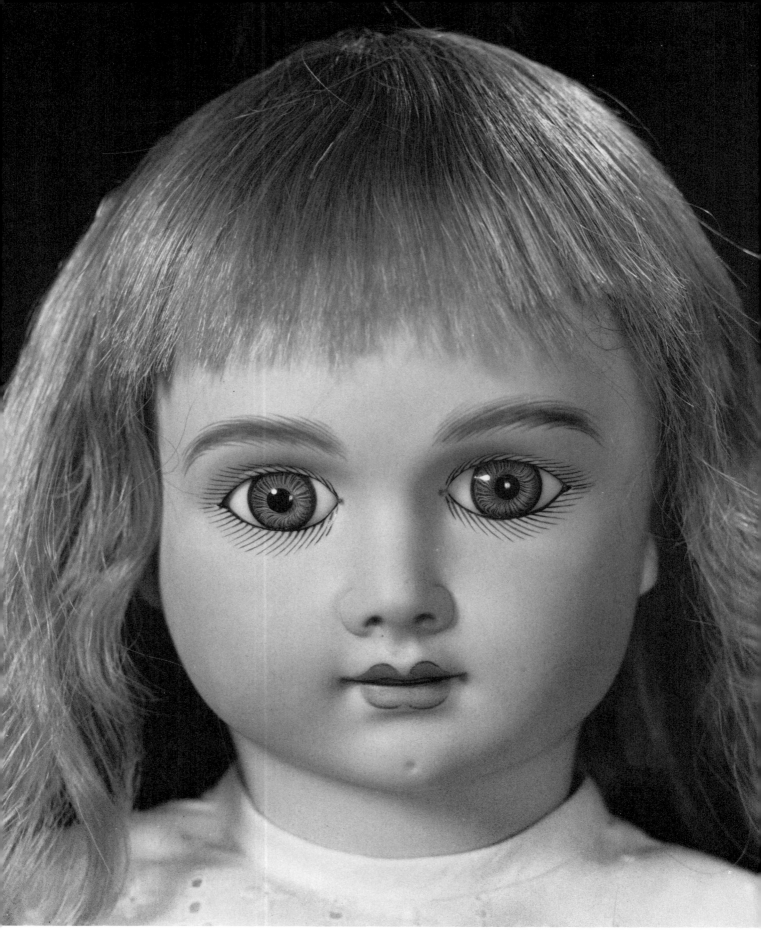

Illustration 11. A 14T.

Illustration 12. Belton.

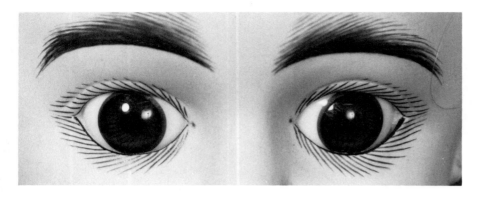 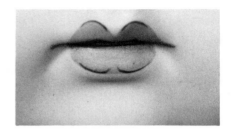

Illustration 13. F. G. in scroll/ eyes, lips.

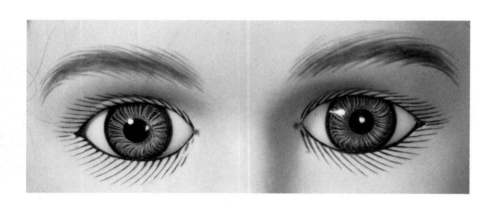 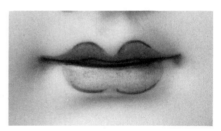

Illustration 14. A 14T/ eyes, lips.

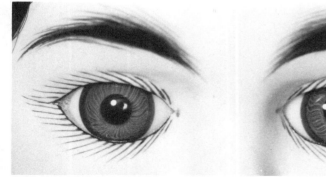 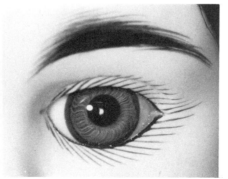 

Illustration 15. Belton/ eyes, lips.

Illustration 16. A. Marque.

Illustration 17. Schmitt.

Illustration 18. *Jumeau D'or.*

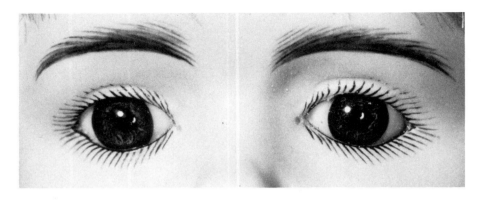
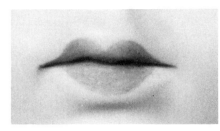

Illustration 19. A. Marque/ eyes, lips.

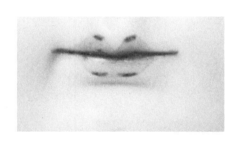

Illustration 20. Schmitt/ eyes, lips.

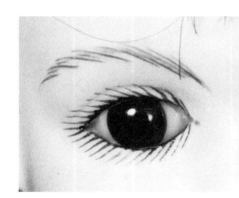

Illustration 21. Jumeau D'or/ eyes, lips.

Let's Practice!

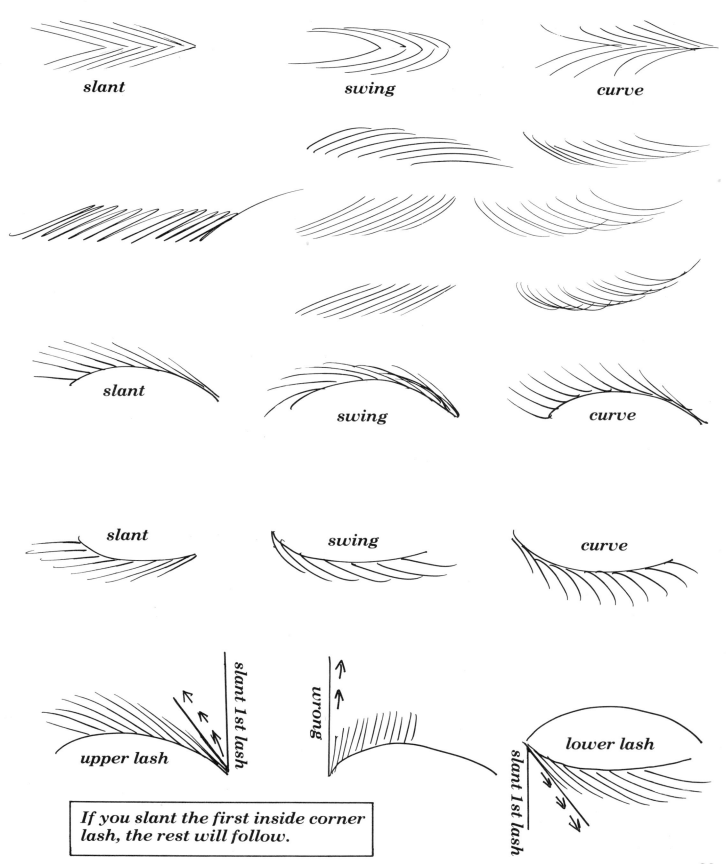

slant *swing* *curve*

slant *swing* *curve*

slant *swing* *curve*

upper lash *slant 1st lash* *wrong* *lower lash* *slant 1st lash*

If you slant the first inside corner lash, the rest will follow.

39

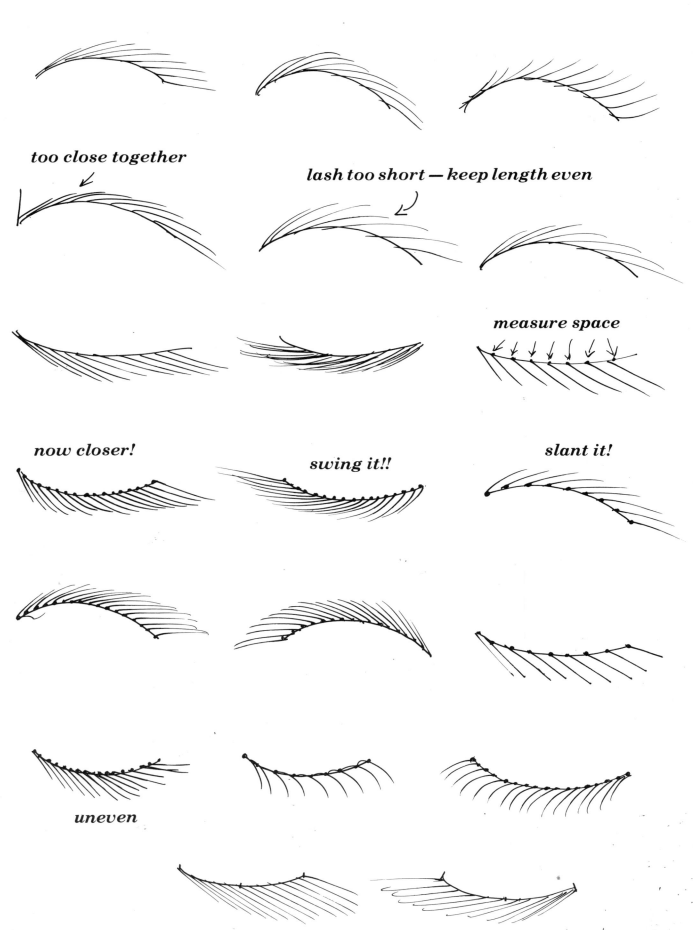

too close together

lash too short — keep length even

measure space

now closer!

swing it!!

slant it!

uneven

Stroking Lashes

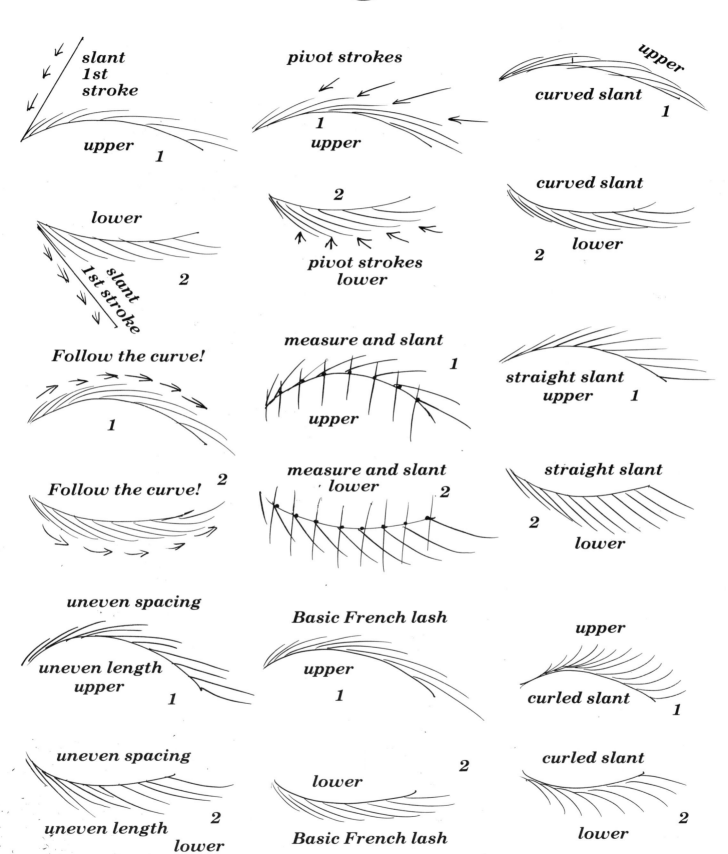

slant
1st
stroke

upper   1

pivot strokes

1
upper

upper

curved slant
1

lower

slant
1st stroke

2

2

pivot strokes
lower

curved slant

lower
2

Follow the curve!

1

measure and slant

1

upper

straight slant
upper   1

Follow the curve!   2

measure and slant
lower
2

straight slant

2

lower

uneven spacing

uneven length
upper

1

Basic French lash

upper

1

upper

curled slant

1

uneven spacing

uneven length
lower

2

lower

2

Basic French lash

curled slant

2

lower

Building A Brow

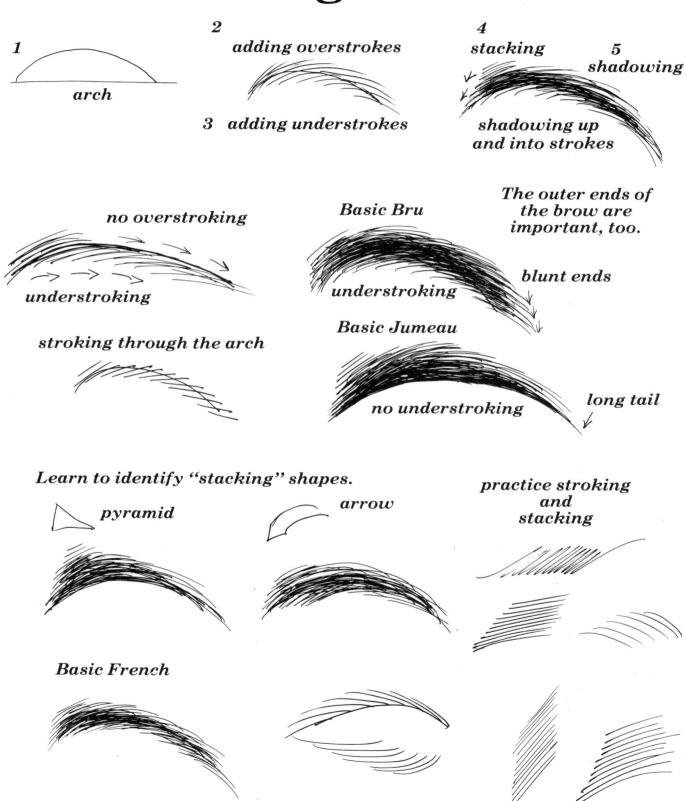

1 arch

2 adding overstrokes

3 adding understrokes

4 stacking

5 shadowing

shadowing up
and into strokes

no overstroking

understroking

stroking through the arch

Basic Bru

understroking

Basic Jumeau

no understroking

The outer ends of
the brow are
important, too.

blunt ends

long tail

Learn to identify "stacking" shapes.

pyramid

arrow

practice stroking
and
stacking

Basic French

Three Basic Brow Shapes

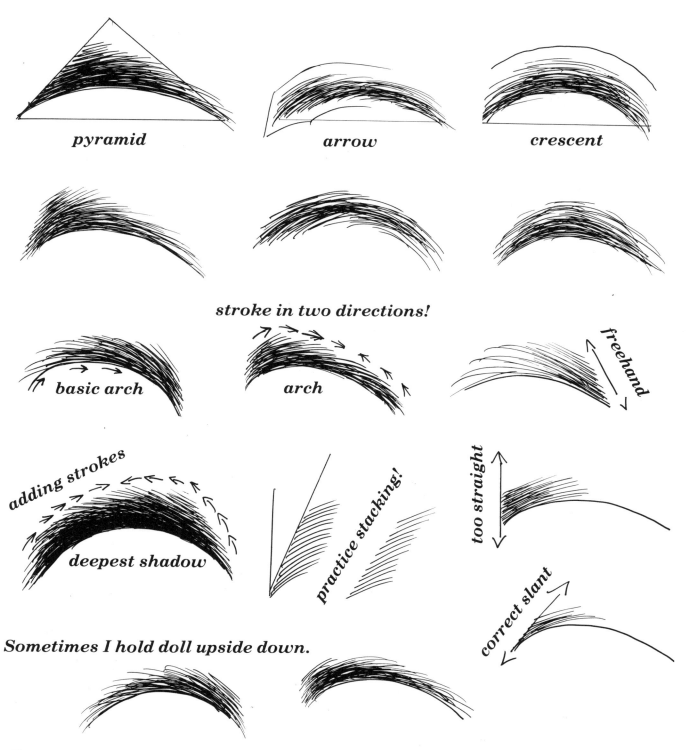

pyramid

arrow

crescent

stroke in two directions!

basic arch

arch

freehand

adding strokes

deepest shadow

practice stacking!

too straight

correct slant

Sometimes I hold doll upside down.

Don't lose your strokes by over shading!

Comparing Angles For Stacking Different Style Brows

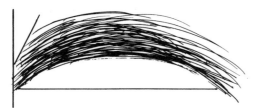

Bru or A.T.

Belton or F.G.

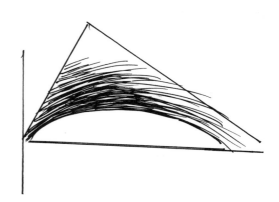

Bru or A.T.

Heavy Jumeau

Heavy Fashion

Lightly stroked Jumeau

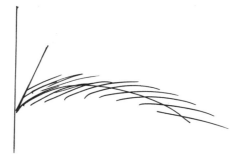

Lightly stroked Fashion

Schmitt

Some Do's and Don'ts

Compare spaces — turn upside down to judge.

Do it free hand.

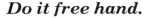

Follow the strokes as you shade the brow.

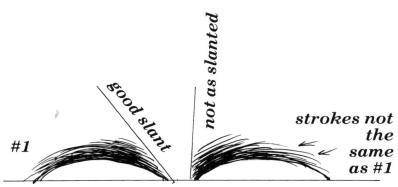

#1   good slant   not as slanted   strokes not the same as #1

Try to slant the stacking alike.

Strokes are lost from over-shadowing.

Shade up into the strokes.

Allow your strokes to show.

average tail

blunt end tail

long tapered tail

Four Popular Styles

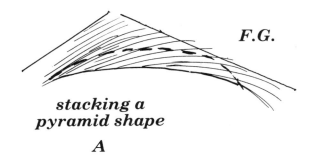

F.G.

*stacking a
pyramid shape*

A

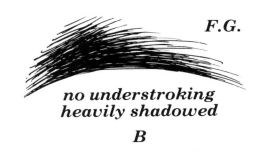

F.G.

*no understroking
heavily shadowed*

B

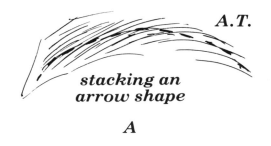

A.T.

*stacking an
arrow shape*

A

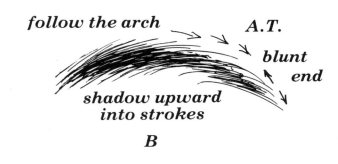

follow the arch **A.T.**

*blunt
end*

*shadow upward
into strokes*

B

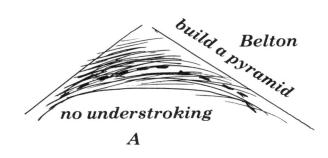

build a pyramid **Belton**

no understroking

A

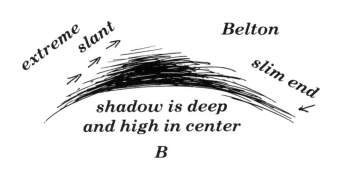

extreme slant **Belton**

slim end

*shadow is deep
and high in center*

B

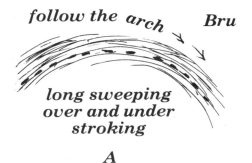

follow the arch **Bru**

*long sweeping
over and under
stroking*

A

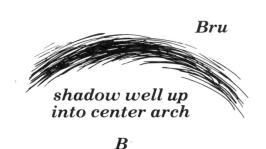

Bru

*shadow well up
into center arch*

B

Lips

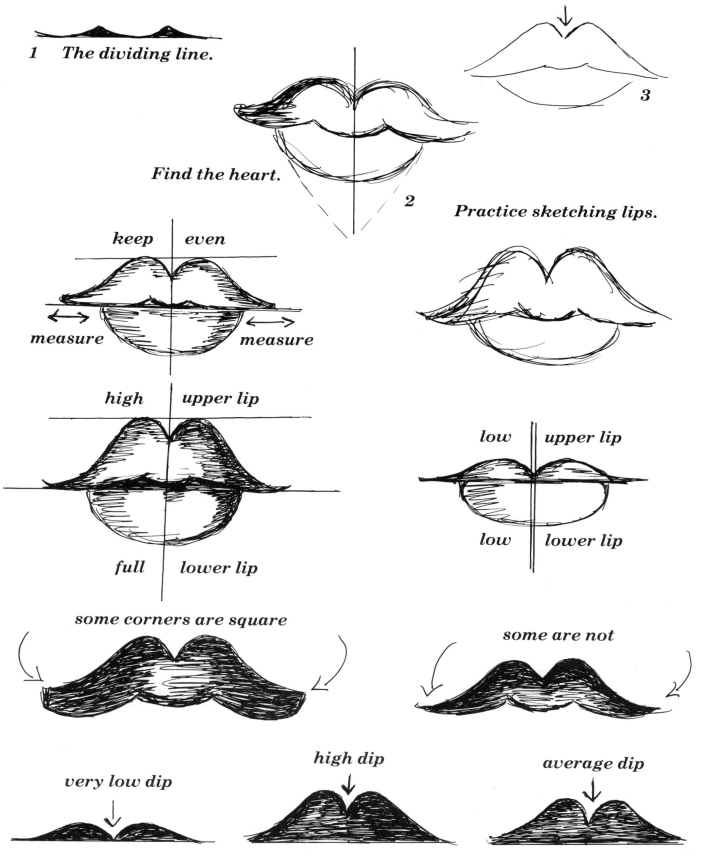

1 **The dividing line.**

Find the heart.

2

3

Practice sketching lips.

keep *even*

←*measure* *measure*→

high *upper lip*

full *lower lip*

low *upper lip*

low *lower lip*

some corners are square

some are not

very low dip

high dip

average dip

47

The More You Sketch, The Easier to Paint!

It's easy to GOOF!

draw imaginary line

look for the heart

48

Illustration 12. *Renoir, Girl With Red Hair: A 14T/ head circumference 13in (33cm), human hair wig, 24in (61cm) tall on ball-jointed body.*

Illustration 13. *Little Prince and Mosser Bear: Bru Jne 13/ head circumference 14in (35.6cm), human hair wig, 28in (71.1cm) tall on ball-jointed body with lower bisque arms. Bear — Marion Mosser Arnold.*

Illustration 14. Little Prince: Bru Jne. 13/ head circumference 14in (36.9cm), human hair wig, 28in (71.1cm) tall on ball-jointed body with lower bisque arms.

Illustration 15. *I Have A New Dress: Steiner FA15: Head circ. 8in (20.3cm) human hair wig. 15in (38.1cm) tall on ball-jointed body.*

Illustration 16. *Steiner FA15: Head circumference 8in (20.3cm), human hair wig, 15in (38.1cm) tall on ball-jointed body.*

Illustration 17. *A. Marque: Head circumference 9½in (24.2cm), human hair wig, 18½in (47cm) tall on ball-jointed body with lower bisque arms.*

Illustration 18. *A Wee One: Bru Jne (unmarked): Head circumference 6½in (16.5cm), dyed lambskin wig, 10in (25.4cm) tall on ball-jointed body. Costume — Neva W. Garnett.*

Illustration 19. *Renoir and Doll: A 14T/ head circumference 13in (33cm), human hair wig, 24in (61cm) tall on ball-jointed body.*

Illustration 20: *Belton Beauty: Head circumference 10in (25.4cm), human hair wig, 18in (45.7cm) tall on ball-jointed body.*

Illustration 21. *All Dressed Up: Bru Jne 10/ head circumference 12in (30.5cm), human hair wig, 24in (61cm) tall on kid body with lower bisque arms and shoulder plate. Costume — Clara Wade.*

Illustration 22. *Fashion Gent (unmarked): Head circumference 8in (20.3cm), human hair wig, 17in (43.2cm) tall on kid body with bisque limbs.*

Illustration 23. Cousins: **Left:** A 14T/ head circumference 8½in (21.6cm), goatskin wig, 14in (35.6cm) tall on ball-jointed body. **Center:** Jumeau (called Lyric) head circumference 9½in (24.2cm), lambskin wig, 16in (40.6cm) tall on ball-jointed body. **Right:** Round face Steiner (unmarked) head circumference 9¾in (24.9cm), lambskin wig, 15in (38.1cm) tall on ball-jointed body.

Illustration 24. *A Hug for Teddy: Bru Jne 11/ head circumference 10¾in (27.4cm), mohair wig, 18in (45.7cm) tall on ball-jointed body. Bear — Aleen Rollins.*

Illustration 25. *Giddyap: A 14T/ head circumference 13in (33cm), synthetic wig, 24in (61cm) tall on ball-jointed body.*

Illustration 26. A Little One: A 8T/ head circumference 6½in (16.5cm), dyed lambskin wig, 10in (25.4cm) tall on ball-jointed body. Costume — Neva W. Garnett.

Illustration 27. *Rock-A-Bye: Bru Jne 8/ head circumference 9½in (24.2cm), human hair wig, 17in (43.2cm) tall on ball-jointed body. Costume — Ann Winters.*

Illustration 28. *Emile' and His China Dog: Bru Jne marked* $\overset{B}{\underset{U}{R}}$ / *head circumference 11½in (29.2cm), mohair wig, 22in (55.9cm) tall on kid body with lower bisque arms. Costume — Clara Workentine.*

Illustration 29. *The Bru Children:* **Left:** *Bru Jne 13/ head circumference 14in (35.6cm), human hair wig, 28in (71.1cm) tall on ball-jointed body with lower bisque arms. Costume — Patty Manuel.* **Right:** *Bru Jne 13/ head circumference 14in (35.6cm), human hair wig, 28in (71.1cm) tall on ball-jointed body with lower bisque arms.*

Illustration 30. *F. G. Fashion (unmarked): Head circumference 8in (20.3cm), dyed lambskin wig, 18in (45.7cm) tall on kid body with bisque limbs.*

Illustration 31. *See My Birdie: Bru Jne 13/ head circumference 14in (35.6cm), human hair wig, 28in (71.1cm) tall on ball-jointed body with lower bisque arms. Costume — Neva W. Garnett.*

Illustration 32. *Bru Jne 13: Head circumference 14in (35.6cm), human hair wig, 28in (71.1cm) tall on ball-jointed body with lower bisque arms.*

Illustration 33. *French Lace: "Smiler" Fashion/ lock-neck flange, head circumference 7in (17.8cm), mohair wig, 16in (40.6cm) tall on kid body with bisque limbs. Costume — Agnes Daisey. Satin and antique French lace.*

Illustration 34. *"Smiler" Fashion/ lock-neck flange, head circumference 7in (17.8cm), mohair wig, 16in (40.6cm) tall on kid body with bisque limbs.*

Illustration 35. *Just Waiting: F. G. in scroll/ head circumference 14in (35.6cm), human hair wig, 26in (66cm) tall on ball-jointed body. Costume — Clara Workentine.*

Illustration 36. *F. G. (scroll): Head circumference 14in (35.6cm), human hair wig, 26in (66cm) tall on ball-jointed body.*

Illustration 37. *Fashion (unmarked): Head circumference 8in (20.3cm), mohair wig, 20in (50.8cm) tall on kid body with bisque arms.*

Illustration 38. *F. G. Fashion (unmarked): Head circumference 8in (20.3cm), mohair wig, 20in (50.8cm) tall on kid body with bisque limbs.*

Illustration 39. *Practicing the Piano:* **Left:** *A 14T/ head circumference 13in (33cm), human hair wig, 24in (61cm) tall on ball-jointed body.* **Right:** *A 14T/ head circumference 13in (33cm), human hair wig, 24in (61cm) tall on ball-jointed body.*

Illustration 40. *Bru Jne 11: Head circumference 11in (27.9cm), human hair wig, 22in (55.9cm) tall on kid body with bisque shoulder plate and limbs.*

Illustration 41. Let's Play: **Left:** Jumeau Bébé/ head circumference 10¾in (27.4cm), human hair wig, 18in (45.7cm) tall on ball-jointed body. **Right:** Round-face Steiner (unmarked) head circumference 9¾in (24.9cm), lambskin wig, 15½in (39.4cm) tall on ball-jointed body.

Illustration 42. *Tête Jumeau/head circumference 14½in (36.9cm), human hair wig, 28in (71.1cm) tall on ball-jointed body.*

Illustration 43. Bru Jne 13: Head circumference 14in (35.6cm), human hair wig, 28in (71.1cm) tall on ball-jointed body with lower bisque arms.

Illustration 44. Sisters: **Left:** *Bru Jne 10/ head circumference 9½in (24.2cm), mohair hair wig, 16in (40.6cm) tall on ball-jointed body.* **Right:** *Bru Jne 8/ head circumference 9¾in (24.9cm) mohair wig, 17in (43.2cm) tall on ball-jointed body. Costume — Hattie.*

Illustration 45. *Laughing Boy and Babette:* **Left:** *SFBJ 238/ character with dimples and freckles. Head circumference 9in (22.9cm), human hair wig, 18in (45.7cm) tall on ball-jointed body.* **Right:** *A 14T/ head circumference 8½in (21.6cm), goatskin wig, 14in (35.6cm) tall on ball-jointed body.*

Illustration 46. *Jumeau D'or Fashion: Head circumference 7½in (19.1cm), human hair wig, 17in (43.2cm) tall on kid body with bisque limbs.*

Illustration 47. *Bébé Schmitt: Head circumference 9in (22.9cm), lambskin wig, 15in (38.1cm) tall on ball-jointed body.*

Illustration 48. *Jumeau Bébé/ with molded teeth: Head circumference 10¾in (27.4cm), human hair wig, 18½in (47cm) tall on ball-jointed body.*

Illustration 49. My Turn!: **Left:** *Bru Jne 10, 10in (25.4cm) tall.* **Right:** *screaming (SFBJ) Jumeau, 12in (30.5cm) tall.*

Illustration 50. *Coquette: Jumeau (called Louve): Head circumference 10in (25.4cm), human hair wig, 18in (45.7cm) tall on ball-jointed body. Costume — fine wool, fox fur muff.*

Illustration 51. *All Dressed Up — Nowhere To Go!* **Left:** *Bru Jne 13/ head circumference 14in (35.6cm), human hair wig, 28in (71.1cm) tall on ball-jointed body with lower bisque arms.* **Right:** *Bru Jne 13/ head circumference 14in (35.6cm), human hair wig, 28in (71.1cm) tall on ball-jointed body with lower bisque arms.*

Illustration 52. *Tea for Two:* **Back:** *Bru Jne 13/ head circumference 14in (35.6cm), human hair wig, 28in (71.1cm) tall on ball-jointed body with lower bisque arms.* **Foreground:** *Bru Jne 13/ head circumference 14in (35.6cm), human hair wig, 28in (71.1cm) tall on ball-jointed body with lower bisque arms.*

Illustration 53. *Ready for Sunday School: A 14T/ head circumference 13in (33cm), human hair wig, 24in (61cm) tall on ball-jointed body.*

Illustration 54. Ready for a Stroll in the Park: **Left:** *Bru Jne 10/ head circumference 6½in (16.5cm), lambskin wig, 10in (25.4cm) tall on ball-jointed body.* **Center:** *F. G. Fashion/ unmarked, head circumference 8in (20.3cm), dyed lambskin, 18in (45.7cm) tall on kid body with bisque limbs.* **Right:** *Bru Jne 10/ head circumference 6½in (16.5cm), dyed lambskin wig, 10in (25.4cm) tall on ball-jointed body.*

Illustration 55. *Girl in Green: Bru Jne 13/ head circumference 14in (35.6cm), synthetic wig, 28in (71.1cm) tall on ball-jointed body with lower bisque arms.*

Illustration 56. *I'm a Good Girl: Bru Jne 13/ head circumference 14in (35.6cm), human hair wig, 28in (71.1cm) tall on ball-jointed body with lower bisque arms.*

Illustration 57. *Haughty Lady: Portrait Jumeau Fashion/ head circumference 8in (20.3cm), human hair wig, 20in (50.8cm) tall on kid body with bisque limbs.*